Make It:
Chocolate

TIME FOR KIDS

Madison Spielman

Consultant

Timothy Rasinski, Ph.D.
Kent State University

Publishing Credits

Dona Herweck Rice, *Editor-in-Chief*

Robin Erickson, *Production Director*

Lee Aucoin, *Creative Director*

Conni Medina, M.A.Ed., *Editorial Director*

Jamey Acosta, *Editor*

Stephanie Reid, *Photo Editor*

Rachelle Cracchiolo, M.S.Ed., *Publisher*

Based on writing from *TIME For Kids.*

TIME For Kids and the *TIME For Kids* logo are registered trademarks of TIME Inc. Used under license.

Teacher Created Materials

5301 Oceanus Drive
Huntington Beach, CA 92649-1030
http://www.tcmpub.com

ISBN 978-1-4333-3621-8

© 2012 by Teacher Created Materials, Inc.

BP 5028

Table of Contents

Chocolate Dreams

Close your eyes and imagine your favorite chocolate **candy**.

Think about how it smells.
Think about the taste. Think
about how it melts in your mouth.

Mmmmm! Are you ready for some chocolate now?

If you are like most people in the United States, you love chocolate, and you eat about twelve pounds of it each year!

Where Does Chocolate Come From?

Cacao (kuh-KAH-oh) comes from the Spanish word that means "food of the gods."

Chocolate is made from the seeds of the **cacao tree**. The seeds grow inside **cacao pods**. They are called *cocoa beans*.

They should really be called **cacao beans**. But long ago, English speaking people spelled the word *cacao* wrong by mistake. People have just kept it that way.

England

Switzerland

Hudson Bay

Labrador Sea

North Atlantic Ocean

North Sea

English Channel

Bay of Biscay

North Atlantic Ocean

Mediterranean Sea

Gulf of Mexico

Caribbean Sea

GHANA   NIGERIA

IVORY COAST

The Equator

BRAZIL

South Atlantic Ocean

Key

where cocoa comes from

where hard chocolate was first made

Most of the world's cocoa beans come from countries in South America, Africa, and Asia. The countries are located near the equator. Look at the map to find them.

The First Chocolate

cacao pod

Chocolate started out a very long time ago as a type of drink made in South America. But hard chocolate that people could eat was not made until much later.

People long ago did not have hard chocolate. Hard chocolate like we have today was not made until 1828.

In that year, a Dutch chemist removed the cocoa butter from cocoa beans. Cocoa butter tastes bitter.

Without the cocoa butter, **cocoa powder** was left. Cocoa powder is the delicious beginning of chocolate.

cacao beans

The first solid chocolate was sold in England in 1847.

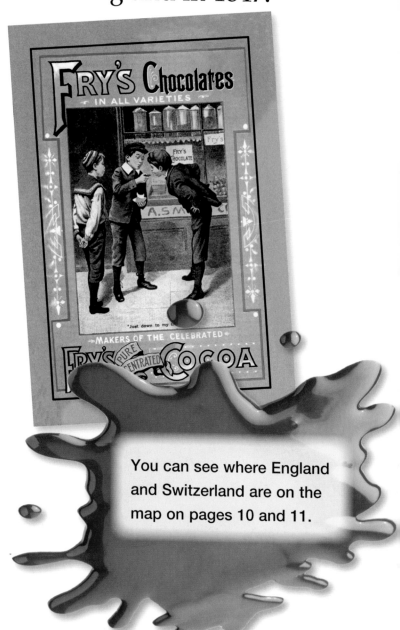

You can see where England and Switzerland are on the map on pages 10 and 11.

dark chocolate

milk chocolate

In 1875, a man from Switzerland added milk to chocolate and made the first milk chocolate. That is the kind of chocolate found in most candy today.

How Is Chocolate Made?

It takes time and work to make good chocolate.

First, the cacao pods must be picked. Then they are **fermented** for six days.

Ferment means to change slowly. Yeast and bacteria can cause this chemical change.

When they are ready, the pods are split open. The seeds are removed and dried.

They are dried in the sun for about seven days. Sometimes they are dried in special machines instead.

Next, the dried beans are sent to chocolate factories.

At the factories, the cocoa butter is removed, and the seeds are roasted and ground into powder.

The powder is mixed with sugar, milk, or other ingredients to make different kinds of chocolate.

Next, the chocolate is heated in a special machine called a **conche**. The best chocolate is heated there for at least one week!

A conche (conch) keeps the chocolate liquid and smooth.

The chocolate is cooled slowly, warmed again, and finally cooled to its final hardness. Now, it is ready to be packaged and sent to stores where you can buy and eat it!

Who Loves Chocolate?

People in the United States eat almost half of all the chocolate eaten in the world.

But it is the Swiss people who love it best. The average person there eats 22 pounds of chocolate each year!

In fact, many people think Swiss chocolate is the best chocolate in the world.

Chocolate, Chocolate Everywhere!

Is chocolate only in candies? No! You can find chocolate in many different foods. Chocolate cake, pudding, cookies, ice cream, and hot cocoa are just a few of them. Wherever you find food, you can probably find some kind of chocolate, too.

What is your favorite chocolate food?

Glossary

cacao beans

cacao pod

cacao tree

candy

cocoa powder

conche

ferment